Tin Can Tracks

Explorer Challenge

Which animal makes these tracks?

OXFORD
UNIVERSITY PRESS

3

4

Retell the Story

Look at the pictures and retell the story in your own words.

Look Back, Explorers

Who helped the children make the tin can stilts?

What are they doing to the tin cans on page 3?

Look at page 9. Why does Floppy look shocked?

Did you find out which animal made these tracks?

What's Next, Explorers?

Now find out about lots of different animal tracks ...

Explorer Challenge
for *Animal Tracks*

What makes these tracks?